United States Government Accountability Office

Testimony

Before the Subcommittee on Aviation, Committee on Transportation and Infrastructure, House of Representatives

For Release on Delivery
Expected at 10:00 a.m. ET
Wednesday, July 23, 2014

I0410935

AVIATION SAFETY

FAA's Efforts to Implement Recommendations to Improve Certification and Regulatory Consistency Face Some Challenges

Statement of Gerald L. Dillingham, Ph.D.
Director, Physical Infrastructure Issues

GAO-14-728T

July 23, 2014

GAO Highlights

Highlights of GAO-14-728T, a testimony before the Subcommittee on Aviation, Committee on Transportation and Infrastructure, House of Representatives

AVIATION SAFETY

FAA's Efforts to Implement Recommendations to Improve Certification and Regulatory Consistency Face Some Challenges

Why GAO Did This Study

Among its responsibilities for aviation safety, FAA issues certificates for new aircraft and parts, and grants approvals for changes to air operations and aircraft, based on federal aviation regulations. Various studies, GAO's prior work, and industry stakeholders have raised questions about the efficiency of FAA's certification and approval processes, as well as the consistency of its staff in interpreting aviation regulations. Over time, FAA has implemented efforts to address these issues, but they persist as FAA faces greater industry demand and its overall workload has increased. The 2012 FAA Modernization and Reform Act required FAA to work with industry to resolve these issues. In response, FAA chartered two committees—one to address certification and approval processes and another to address regulatory consistency—which recommended improvements in 2012. In 2013, FAA published an implementation plan for addressing the certification and approval process recommendations and promised to publish an implementation plan for addressing the regulatory consistency recommendations at a later date.

This testimony provides information on FAA's progress in implementing the (1) certification and approval process recommendations and (2) regulatory consistency recommendations. It also discusses future challenges industry stakeholders believe FAA will face in implementing these recommendations. This testimony is based on GAO products issued from 2010 to 2014, updated in July 2014 through reviews of recent FAA and industry documents and interviews of FAA officials and industry representatives.

View GAO-14-728T. For more information, contact Gerald L. Dillingham, Ph. D. at (202) 512-2834 or dillinghamg@gao.gov.

What GAO Found

The Federal Aviation Administration's (FAA) Aircraft Certification Service (Aircraft Certification) is responsible for addressing the certification and approval process recommendations, and has made progress. Aircraft Certification is implementing and has set milestones for completing 14 initiatives, several of which were originally begun as part of earlier certification process improvement efforts. The initiatives range from developing a comprehensive road map for major change initiatives, to improving Aircraft Certification's process for prioritizing requests for certifications and approvals (project sequencing), to reorganizing the small aircraft certification regulation. According to an update prepared by FAA in May 2014, one initiative has been completed and most are on track to be completed within 3 years. However, according to this update, two initiatives will not meet planned milestones, including the one for improving FAA's program for delegating authority to organizations to carry out some certification activities. Also, a third initiative for improving consistency of regulatory interpretation was at risk of not meeting planned milestones. Two additional initiatives, while on track for meeting planned milestones in May 2014, faced challenges because of opposition by FAA's labor unions, including one for improving Aircraft Certification's project sequencing process. GAO found in October 2013 that Aircraft Certification continued to lack performance measures for many of these initiatives, a condition that persists. In 2010, GAO had previously recommended that FAA develop a continuous evaluative process with performance goals and measures. FAA agreed but has not yet fully addressed the recommendation. Aircraft Certification officials discussed plans to develop metrics in three phases, beginning in July 2014 and in the future, for measuring (1) the progress of implementing the initiatives throughout FAA, (2) the outcomes of each initiative, and (3) the return on investment for FAA and the industry resulting from implementing the initiatives as a whole.

FAA's Flight Standards Service (Flight Standards) is responsible for addressing the regulatory consistency recommendations, is finalizing plans to do so. FAA has not published a detailed plan with milestones and performance metrics, and officials told GAO that they intend to publish a plan by August 2014. Flight Standards officials said they were making progress in addressing the committee's top priority recommendation—mapping all FAA policy and guidance to relevant federal aviation regulations and developing an electronic system that maintains this information and that is accessible by FAA and industry users. As part of this effort, officials told GAO that Flight Standards has begun eliminating obsolete guidance and linking existing policy and guidance to the regulations.

Going forward, Aircraft Certification's and Flight Standards' efforts may face challenges that could affect successful implementation of the committees' recommendations. Many of these recommendations represent a significant shift in how FAA normally conducts business, and if the workforce is reluctant to implement such changes, FAA's planned initiatives for addressing the recommendations could be delayed. Also, the fact that FAA has not yet implemented performance measures for most of the initiatives is a concern for both GAO and the industry. As GAO concluded in October 2013, without performance measures, FAA will be unable to gather the appropriate data to evaluate the success of current and future initiatives.

_____ **United States Government Accountability Office**

Chairman LoBiondo, Ranking Member Larsen, and Members of the Subcommittee:

I appreciate the opportunity to testify today on the status of the Federal Aviation Administration's (FAA) efforts to improve its certification and approval processes. As you know, FAA is responsible for aviation safety, and part of this responsibility entails issuing certificates for new aircraft and aircraft parts and equipment and granting approvals for such things as changes to air operations and aircraft, based on federal aviation regulations. FAA's current efforts to improve these processes are aimed at (1) improving its decision-making process for issuing certificates and approvals, (2) keeping pace with emerging technology, and (3) enabling industry growth and innovation. Studies published since 1980,[1] our prior work,[2] industry stakeholders, and experts have long raised questions about the efficiency of FAA's certification and approval processes and varying interpretations and applications of its regulations in making certification and approval decisions. More recently, several aviation industry groups have asserted that these issues persist, resulting in delays and higher costs for their members. These delays have been generally attributed to heavy staff workloads and a lack of staff resources to begin new work on certifications and approvals. With greater industry demand and the introduction of new aircraft, equipment, and technology into the national aviation system, FAA's workload has increased and is expected to grow further over the next decade. We previously concluded that it will be critical for FAA to follow through with reforms to its certification and approval processes to meet industry's future needs.[3]

[1] See National Academy of Sciences, *Improving Aircraft Safety: FAA Certification of Commercial Passenger Aircraft*, National Research Council, Committee on FAA Airworthiness Certification Procedures (Washington, D.C.: June 1980); Booz Allen & Hamilton, *Challenge 1000: Recommendations for Future Aviation Safety Regulations* (McLean, VA: Apr. 19, 1996); RTCA Task Force 4, *Final Report of the RTCA Task Force 4 "Certification"* (Washington, D.C.: Feb. 26, 1999; and Independent Review Team Appointed by Secretary of Transportation Mary E. Peters, *Managing Risks in Civil Aviation: A Review of FAA's Approach to Safety* (Washington, D.C.: Sept. 2, 2008).

[2] See GAO, *Aviation Safety: Certification and Approval Processes Are Generally Viewed as Working Well, but Better Evaluative Information Needed to Improve Efficiency*, GAO-11-14 (Washington, D.C.: Oct. 7, 2010) and GAO, *Aircraft Certification: New FAA Approach Needed to Meet Challenges of Advanced Technology*, GAO/RCED-93-155 (Washington, D.C.: Sept. 1993).

[3] GAO, *Aviation Safety: Status of Recommendations to Improve FAA's Certification and Approval Processes*. GAO-14-142T (Washington, D.C.: Oct. 30, 2013).

Over time, FAA has initiated various efforts and initiatives to improve its certification and approval processes and interpret regulations more consistently, including efforts in response to findings and recommendations we made in 2010.[4] However, to bring further attention to these issues and spur additional action, Congress included the following requirements for FAA in the FAA Modernization and Reform Act of 2012:[5] (1) work with the industry to assess and recommend improvements to the certification and approval processes (Section 312) and (2) address the findings from our 2010 report related to FAA interpreting regulations more consistently (Section 313). To meet these requirements, FAA chartered two aviation rulemaking committees in April 2012—the Aircraft Certification Process Review and Reform Aviation Rulemaking Committee (Certification Process Committee) and the Consistency of Regulatory Interpretation Aviation Rulemaking Committee (Regulatory Consistency Committee)—which made recommendations to FAA in May 2012 and November 2012, respectively. In an October 2013 statement, we made preliminary assessments of the two committees' recommendations and FAA's responses,[6] finding that both FAA-chartered committees took reasonable approaches in their work and made relevant, clear, and actionable recommendations to FAA. However, we also discussed challenges to making further improvements to the certification and approval processes, most notably that FAA has not developed performance metrics for measuring the outcomes of the initiatives.[7] In 2010, GAO made two recommendations requiring, among other things, that FAA develop a continuous evaluative process with performance goals and measures for assessing its actions to improve the efficiency of

---

[4]GAO-11-14.

[5]Pub. L. No. 112-95, §§ 312 and 313, 126 Stat. 11, 66 and 67 (2012).

[6]GAO-14-142T.

[7]GAO-14-142T.

its certification and approval processes, and a method to track submission approvals.[8]

This testimony discusses FAA's continuing efforts related to its certification and approval processes. More specifically, it provides information on (1) FAA's progress in implementing the Certification Process Committee recommendations, (2) its progress in implementing the Regulatory Consistency Committee recommendations, and (3) future challenges that others and we identified that FAA faces in implementing these recommendations. This statement is primarily drawn from several GAO products issued since 2010.[9] We have updated the information in July 2014 related to our previous work on the certification and approval processes through a review of more recent FAA and industry documents, including the committees' reports to FAA, FAA's reports to Congress in response to the committees' recommendations as well as additional government and industry documents and reports related to this topic. This review included the May 2012 Certification Process Committee's and the November 2012 Regulatory Consistency Committee's report to FAA; FAA's August 2012 and July 2013 reports to Congress on the results and plan for implementing recommendations made; and FAA's implementation plans to address the committees' recommendations. We also conducted interviews with FAA officials and industry stakeholders—including Boeing, the largest U.S. aircraft manufacturer—and representatives from all eight trade associations that participated in the two aviation rulemaking committees. Related GAO products are footnoted throughout the statement. The reports and testimonies cited in this statement contain detailed explanations of the methods used to conduct

---

[8]GAO-11-14. Specifically, we recommended that FAA develop a continuous evaluative process and use it to create measurable performance goals for the actions, track performance toward those goals, and determine appropriate process changes. We also recommended that FAA develop and implement a process in Flight Standards to track how long certification and approval submissions are wait-listed, the reasons for wait-listing them, and the factors that eventually allowed initiation of the certification process. FAA partially addressed the first recommendation and fully addressed the other.

[9]GAO-11-14; GAO, *Aviation Safety: Additional FAA Efforts Could Enhance Safety Risk Management*, GAO-12-898 (Washington, D.C.: Sept. 12, 2012); GAO, *Aviation: Status of DOT's Actions to Address the Future of Aviation Advisory Committee's Recommendations*, GAO-13-657 (Washington, D.C.: July 25, 2013); GAO-142T; GAO, *FAA Reauthorization Act: Progress and Challenges Implementing Various Provisions of the 2012 Act*, GAO-14-285T (Washington, D.C.: Feb. 5, 2014); and GAO, *Aviation Safety: Additional Oversight Planning by FAA Could Enhance Safety Risk Management*, GAO-14-516 (Washington, D.C.: June 25, 2014).

our prior work. We provided a draft of the new information contained in this statement to the Department of Transportation (DOT) for technical review and addressed its views in the body of our statement where appropriate.

The work upon which this testimony is based was conducted in accordance with generally accepted government auditing standards. Those standards require that we plan and perform the audit to obtain sufficient, appropriate evidence to provide a reasonable basis for our findings and conclusions based on our audit objectives. We believe that the evidence obtained provides a reasonable basis for our findings and conclusions based on our audit objectives.

Background

Located in FAA's Office of Aviation Safety (Aviation Safety), the Aircraft Certification Service (Aircraft Certification) and Flight Standards Service (Flight Standards) issue certificates and approvals for new aviation products to be used in the national airspace system as well as for new operators in the system, such as air carriers, based on federal aviation regulations (see fig. 1 below). FAA inspectors and engineers interpret and implement these regulations governing certificates and approvals through FAA policies and guidance, including orders, notices, and advisory circulars. Additionally, FAA also has the authority to use private individuals and organizational entities, known as designees, to carry out many certification activities on behalf of the FAA Administrator in order to enable FAA to better concentrate its limited staff resources on safety-critical functions.[10]

---

[10]Administered under 14 C.F.R. Part 183, FAA has the authority to designate private individuals to act as representatives of the agency for examining, inspecting, and testing persons and aircraft for the purpose of issuing certificates. In 2005, FAA established the organization designation authorization program to consolidate all existing organizational delegation types into this single program. 70 Fed. Reg. 59946, Oct. 13, 2005.

Figure 1: Federal Aviation Administration's Organizational Structure for Processing Certificates and Approvals

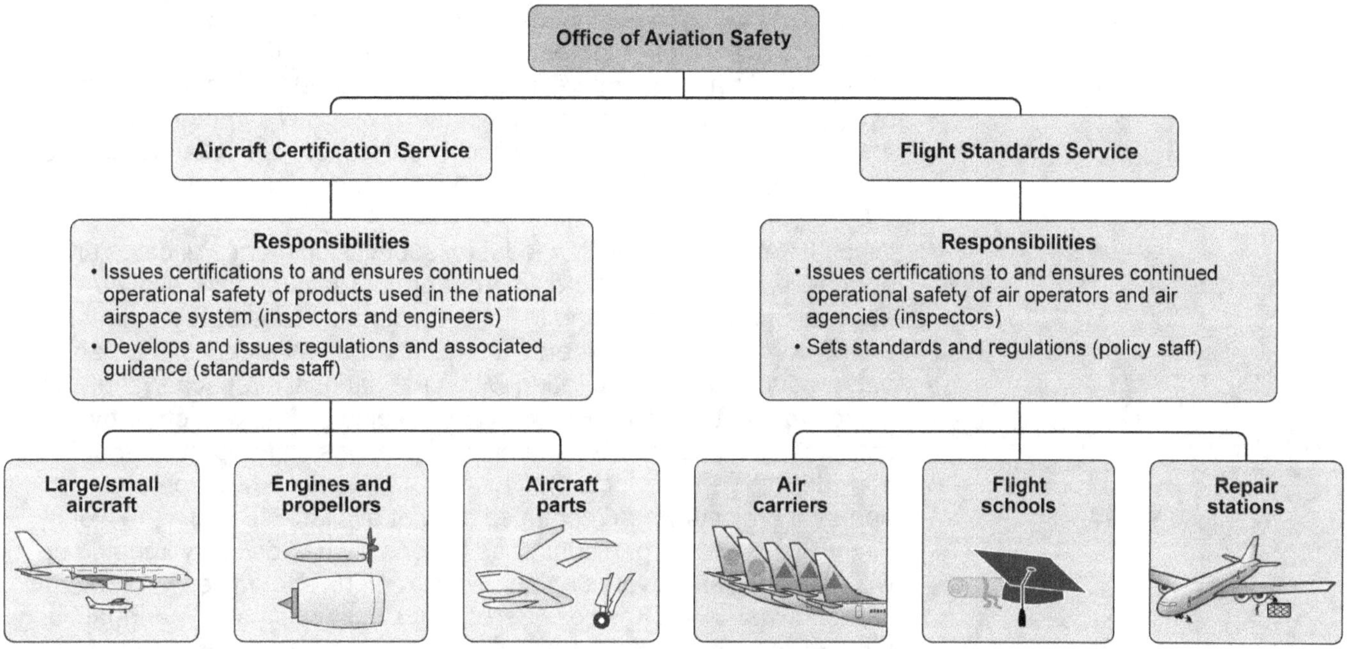

Source: GAO presentation of FAA information. | GAO-14-728T

Note: The Flight Standards Service's oversight responsibilities include air operators (e.g., air carriers and air taxi services) and air agencies (e.g., flight schools and repair stations).

In Aircraft Certification, approximately 880 engineers and inspectors issue certifications and approvals to the designers and manufacturers of new aircraft and aircraft engines, propellers, parts, and equipment, including the avionics and other equipment required for modernizing the air traffic control system under the Next Generation Air Transportation System (NextGen).[11] Since 2005, Aircraft Certification has used a project sequencing system to nationally prioritize certification submissions on the basis of available resources. In fiscal year 2013, Aircraft Certification issued 3,496 design approvals, 57 production approvals, and 536 airworthiness certificates.

---

[11]NextGen is a federal effort to transform the U.S. national airspace system from a ground-based system of air traffic control to a satellite-based system of air traffic management.

In Flight Standards, approximately 4,000 inspectors issue certificates and approvals allowing individuals and entities to operate in the national airspace system. These include certificates to commercial air carriers, operators of smaller commercial aircraft, repair stations, and flight training schools and training centers. Flight Standards field office managers in over 100 field offices initiate certification projects within their offices on a first-come, first served basis. In fiscal year 2013, Flight Standards issued 259 air operator certificates and 159 air agency certificates.

When FAA receives aviation industry submissions for certificates and approvals, it must determine whether or not resources are available to begin the project. According to FAA, the agency considers its highest priority to be overseeing the continued operational safety of the people and products already operating within the national airspace system. The same staff that provide this oversight are also tasked with other oversight activities, such as processing new certifications and approvals that FAA considers to be lower priority. FAA wait-lists new certification and approval projects when resources are not available to begin the work. Flight Standards, in particular, has historically had difficulty keeping up with its certification workload across its regions and offices, a problem that persists.[12] FAA has considered ways to supplement its annual budget by expanding its sources of funding to deal with its increasing workload and staff shortages. However, FAA has limited options as it cannot levy fees on its customers for most of the services it provides to industry, including aviation product certifications and approvals.[13]

Attempts have been made to provide FAA with additional funding from industry stakeholders for processing certifications and approvals. In 2007, the administration submitted a reauthorization proposal to Congress that called for major changes to FAA's funding and budget structure. These changes were intended to provide a more stable, reliable basis for funding in the long term, in part by allowing FAA to impose fees on

---

[12]According to a recent DOT's Office of Inspector General (OIG) report, as of October 2013, Flight Standards faced a significant backlog of aviation certification applications, with 138 applicants wait-listed for more than 3 years. See DOT OIG, *Weak Processes Have Led to A Backlog of Flight Standards Certification Applications*, Federal Aviation Administration, Report Number AV-2014-056 (Washington, D.C.: June 12, 2014).

[13]Congress has historically prohibited FAA from collecting additional funding through the implementation of new aviation user fees. The latest prohibition is contained in the Consolidated Appropriations Act, 2014, Pub. L. No. 113-76, 128 Stat. 5, 578 (2014).

manufacturers for the various activities and costs related to aircraft certification and approval. Congress has previously authorized other agencies to charge these types of "user fees" for services rendered for processing product certification and approval. For example, the Medical Device User Fee and Modernization Act of 2002 authorized the Food and Drug Administration (FDA) to charge and retain a fee for providing services related to reviewing medical device products.[14] However, this broad authority has not been granted to FAA.

Most FAA Initiatives to Improve Its Aircraft Certification and Approval Process Are on Track

In May 2012, the Certification Process Committee made six recommendations to Aircraft Certification to streamline and reengineer the product certification and approval processes, improve efficiency and effectiveness within Aircraft Certification, and redirect resources for support of certification. The Certification Process Committee further recommended that FAA develop measures of effectiveness for its activities and a means of tracking its progress. In August 2012, FAA reported its plan to Congress for addressing the Certification Process Committee's recommendations, and, in July 2013, the agency issued an implementation plan with 14 initiatives. FAA updated this plan in January 2014 and plans to issue further updates on the status of the initiatives periodically.[15]

Most Initiatives Are on Track for Meeting Planned Completion Milestones

Since the January update, Aircraft Certification has continued its efforts to address the recommendations to improve its certification and approval processes and is implementing the 14 initiatives. These initiatives touch on various aspects of Aircraft Certification's work and, according to FAA several predate the committee's recommendations and were part of on-going continuous efforts to address long-standing certification issues and to improve the certification process. The initiatives range from developing a comprehensive road map for major change initiatives, to improving the

---

[14]FDA reviews applications from manufacturers that wish to market medical devices in the United States. To facilitate prompt approval of new devices and clearance of devices that are substantially equivalent to those legally on the market, Congress passed the Act to authorize FDA to collect user fees from manufacturers. In return, the Act requires FDA to meet performance goals tied to the agency's review process. Pub. L. No. 107-250, 116 Stat. 1588 (2002).

[15]FAA, *Detailed Implementation Plan for the Federal Aviation Administration Modernization and Reform Act of 2012, Pub. L. No. 112-95, Section 312*, Jan. 31, 2014.

project sequencing process, to reorganizing the small aircraft certification regulation.[16] Figure 2, based on an interim May 2014 update that FAA provided to us, summarizes FAA's determination of the status of the 14 initiatives.

---

[16]14 C.F.R. Part 23. In June 2013, a joint FAA-industry committee recommended to FAA changes to part 23. According to FAA officials, FAA will devise a plan to implement the recommendations and initiate new rulemaking for part 23 in 2015.

Figure 2: Status of the Federal Aviation Administration's Certification Process Initiatives (Section 312), as of May 2014

Initiatives	Year 2011	2012	2013	2014	2015	2016	2017
Develop roadmap for change initiatives			On track through early 2014				
Deploy tracking system for certification initiatives		Complete 2012					
Improve effectiveness of organization designation authorization (ODA) program[a]	At risk 2011–2014			On track / future			
Develop FAA auditing training for ODA oversight			At risk 2013–2014	future			
Expand delegation for approving instructions for continued airworthiness[b] to ODA		On track 2012–2014		future			
Expand delegation for approving aircraft emissions data to ODA		On track 2012–2014		future			
Expand delegation for approving aircraft noise compliance to ODA		On track 2012–2014		future			
Improve project sequencing process	On track 2011–2014			future			
Update 14 C.F.R. Part 21[c]		On track 2012–2014		future			
Improve validation process[d]		On track 2012–2014		future			
Streamline process for adopting mandatory international airworthiness information[e]		At risk 2012–2014		future (no due date)			
Expedite rulemaking process		On track 2012–2014		future			
Reorganize 14 C.F.R. Part 23[f]	At risk 2011–2014			future			
Improve consistency of regulatory interpretations[g]		On track 2012–2014					

Legend:
- Complete
- On track or on schedule
- At risk of getting off track or off schedule
- Will not meet planned milestone
- Future completion

Source: GAO presentation of FAA information. | GAO-14-728T

Note: Future completion shown in the figure indicates when an initiative is planned to be completed.

[a]FAA delegates authority to organizations under the organization designation authorization program to carry out certain functions on behalf of the agency.

[b]Instructions for continued airworthiness include such things as maintenance manuals and inspection programs for maintaining operational safety of aviation products.

[c]14 C.F.R. Part 21 is the regulation under which aircraft products and parts are certificated.

[d]The validation process is a form of certification to establish compliance for airplanes designed outside their countries in order to issue a type certificate for these airplanes.

[e]No due date has been assigned to this initiative.

[14 C.F.R. Part 23 is the regulation under which small airplanes are certificated.

[9]This initiative is on hold until issuance of the implementation plan for addressing recommendations to improve regulatory consistency.

According to the May 2014 update that FAA provided to us, 1 of the 14 initiatives has been completed, and 10 initiatives are on track for completion within planned time frames. FAA deployed a tracking system to monitor the implementation of the initiatives in June 2013, but the agency indicated it is still finalizing the mechanisms for authorizing staff with the appropriate level of review and approval rights in the system. Also, ten of the initiatives were on track for meeting their planned completion milestones. For example, the initiatives to expand the authority for approving aircraft emissions data and noise compliance under the organization designation authorization (ODA) program are on track to be completed in 2015.[17] In addition, the initiative to expedite rulemaking by, among other things, adopting a rulemaking prioritization tool to update airworthiness standards for special conditions is scheduled to be completed in September of this year.[18] Further, three of the initiatives were in danger of getting off track between 2011 and 2013 and are now back on schedule.

Some Initiatives Will Not Meet or Are at Risk of Not Meeting Planned Milestones

Although most initiatives are on track, according to FAA's May 2014 interim update, 2 of the 14 initiatives will not meet planned milestones:

- *Improve effectiveness of the ODA program:* FAA and two aviation industry groups—the Aerospace Industries Association and General Aviation Manufacturers Association[19]—developed a plan to improve the effectiveness of the ODA process, which is used to authorize organizations to act on behalf of FAA in conducting some safety certification work. In conjunction with the plan, FAA revised the order

[17]FAA grants ODAs for several types of certifications and approvals, including production certificates, parts manufacturer approvals, and type certificates. Some companies, such as Boeing, are granted ODA status for more than one type of certification or approval.

[18]FAA issues special conditions to address new and novel design features during the aircraft certification process.

[19]The Aerospace Industries Association represents major U.S. aerospace and defense manufacturers and suppliers, and the General Aviation Manufacturers Association represents leading global manufacturers of general aviation airplanes and rotorcraft, engines, avionics, and components.

that outlines the new ODA procedures.[20] However, this initiative was purposely delayed to provide industry with additional time to adapt to the changes in the ODA procedures. Representatives of three industry associations we interviewed for this testimony supported the use and expansion of ODA by FAA. In contrast, while the Professional Aviation Safety Specialists (PASS) agrees with the concept of ODA, it has concerns related to expanding the program because representatives contend that oversight of the program requires significant FAA resources.[21] PASS also contends that due to current staffing shortages and increased workload, FAA does not have enough inspectors and engineers to provide the proper surveillance of the designees who would be granted this additional delegation authority. On May 14, 2014, the DOT OIG announced a review of FAA's oversight of the ODA program. The OIG plans to assess FAA's (1) process for determining staffing levels for ODA oversight and (2) oversight of delegated organizations' program controls.

- *Update 14 C.F.R. Part 21:* FAA chartered another aviation rulemaking committee in October 2012 to evaluate improvements to the effectiveness and efficiency of certification procedures for aircraft products and parts,[22] along with incorporating new safety management system (SMS) concepts into the design and manufacturing environment.[23] The committee submitted its report to FAA in July 2014. FAA indicated that the government shutdown in October 2013 delayed some of the actions that the agency had planned to move this effort into the rulemaking process, including submission of the application for rulemaking. According to FAA,

---

[20]FAA Order 8100.15B, change 1, *Organization Designation Authorization Procedures,* Feb. 3, 2014.

[21]PASS is the labor union that represents some of FAA's inspector workforce, among others.

[22]Title 14 of the Code of Federal Regulations Part 21, *Certification Procedures for Products and Parts,* is the basis for evaluating and certifying aircraft, engines, and propellers. The steps in the certification process include the applicant's conceptual design, the application for design approval, definition of the design standards, plans to demonstrate the design meets those standards, generation and substantiation of compliance data, determination of compliance, and issuance of the type certificate.

[23]SMS is a formalized process that involves collecting and analyzing data on aviation operations to identify emerging safety problems, determining risk severity, and mitigating that risk to an acceptable level. This approach to aviation safety is becoming the standard throughout global aviation industry. See GAO-14-516 and GAO-12-898.

however, this delay will have no effect on completion of the final rule, which is planned for 2017.

According to FAA's May 2014 update, 1 of the 14 initiatives was at risk of not meeting planned milestones, which increases the risk that FAA will miss its established implementation time frames for the initiative for addressing its associated recommendation.

- *Improve consistency of regulatory interpretations:* The May 2014 interim update also indicated that the initiative for improving the consistency of regulatory interpretation is at risk of getting off track or off schedule. This initiative responds to the Regulatory Consistency Committee's recommendations for improving the consistency of regulatory interpretation within both Aircraft Certification and Flight Standards. However, Aircraft Certification is relying on Flight Standards to complete the implementation plan for addressing the recommendations. Therefore, Aircraft Certification has placed this initiative on hold. (The next section of this statement discusses in more detail FAA's response to the Regulatory Consistency Committee's recommendations.)

In addition, FAA officials told us that implementation of 2 of the 14 initiatives, while shown as being on track for meeting planned milestones in the May 2014 interim update, face challenges because of opposition by FAA labor unions:

- *Improve project sequencing process:*[24] According to the interim May 2014 update that FAA provided to us, this initiative was listed as on track. However, FAA officials told us the status for this initiative will change to "will not meet planned milestone" in the next revision of the implementation plan expected in July 2014. They explained the change in status is a result of their not expecting to obtain concurrence from the National Air Traffic Controllers Association (NATCA), which represents Aircraft Certification's engineers, among others, on the proposed process changes until December of this year. NATCA has expressed concerns about FAA's plans to change the project sequencing process. The group recommended to FAA that instead of continuing with project sequencing, it should institute a

---

[24]As previously mentioned, Aircraft Certification instituted a sequencing program in 2005 to prioritize the processing of all new certification and approval applications based on the availability of its resources.

system that manages projects locally on a first-come first-served basis, except for projects that fix an unsafe condition. FAA plans to implement the new process, assess its effectiveness, and modify as necessary, and issue the order for all Aircraft Certification offices' project sequencing by December 2016.

- *Expand delegation authority for approving instructions for continued airworthiness (ICA)[25] to ODA:* Similarly, in May 2014, FAA characterized the initiative as on track for meeting the planned milestones, but FAA officials told us this initiative may face challenges as well. The Certification Process Committee noted that the volume of ICAs is rapidly increasing and that ICA delegation is underutilized, and recommended that FAA delegate some ICA review activity to improve and streamline the certification process. However, in December 2013, PASS presented a white paper to FAA that outlined its concerns and reasons it considers this to be a high-risk area that is critical to maintaining adequate safety and aircraft maintenance. PASS strongly disagreed with FAA's plan to expand delegation of ICAs and the Certification Process Committee's decision for making this recommendation. In response, in April 2014, FAA sent a memorandum to PASS to address the concerns and questions contained in the PASS white paper, as well as justify moving forward on the initiative. A PASS representative we interviewed for this testimony told us that PASS continues to have concerns about FAA'S expansion of the ODA program. FAA considers this issue to be resolved with PASS and has decided to go forward with the initiative.

Most Certification Process Improvement Initiatives Lack Measures of Effectiveness

As of May 2014, FAA had not developed metrics for measuring the effectiveness of 9 of the 14 initiatives it has undertaken, nor has it determined metrics to measure the effectiveness of its actions as a whole. According to FAA officials, they plan to develop these metrics in three phases. For the first phase, to be included in the July 2014 update of its implementation plan, FAA will include metrics to measure the progress of the implementation of the initiatives. For the second phase, FAA plans to subsequently develop metrics for measuring the outcomes of each initiative. For the third phase, working with the Aerospace Industries Association, FAA plans to develop metrics for measuring the

---

[25]ICAs include such things as maintenance manuals and inspection programs that are necessary for maintaining the continued operational safety of aviation products, such as aircraft, and aircraft parts and equipment.

global return on investment in implementing all of the initiatives, to the extent that such measurement is possible. We believe that this plan for establishing performance measures is reasonable.

FAA Has Made Some Progress in Addressing Recommendations to Improve the Consistency of Its Regulatory Interpretations, but Details Are Unclear

Unlike FAA's efforts to improve the certification process, although FAA has made some progress towards addressing the regulatory consistency recommendations, the details remain unclear about how FAA will structure its efforts. In November 2012, the Regulatory Consistency Committee made six recommendations to Aircraft Certification and Flight Standards to improve (1) the consistency in how regulations are applied and (2) communications between FAA and industry stakeholders. In July 2013, FAA reported to Congress on its plans for addressing the regulatory consistency recommendations, and included its preliminary plan for determining the feasibility of implementing these recommendations. The report also indicated that FAA would develop a detailed implementation plan that would include an implementation strategy, assign responsibilities to offices and staff, establish milestones, and measure effectiveness for tracking purposes. We found in February 2014 that FAA expected to publish such a detailed implementation plan by late June 2014, more than 6 months after its initial target date of December 2013.[26] In June 2014, FAA officials told us that the implementation plan was under review within FAA and estimated that the agency would issue its detailed plan in August 2014.

Until this detailed plan is released, the specific initiatives for addressing the recommendations are unknown; thus, we cannot analyze information on the status of any planned efforts similar to the information we provided above for the certification process initiatives. Further, FAA's July 2013 preliminary plan does not specify how FAA plans to measure the effectiveness of the initiatives. FAA indicated that "although there may not be any baseline for each recommendation against which to compare improvements, FAA intends to consider: (1) identifying metrics, (2) gathering and developing baseline data, and (3) periodically measuring any changes, positive or negative, in rates of completion." FAA officials provided the following information on how the agency is planning to respond to the six recommendations.

---

[26]GAO-14-285T.

| A Master Source Guidance System | The Regulatory Consistency Committee recommended that Aircraft Certification and Flight Standards (1) review all guidance documents and interpretations to identify and cancel outdated material and electronically link the remaining materials to its applicable rule, and (2) to consolidate Aircraft Certification's and Flight Standards' electronic guidance libraries into a master source guidance system, organized by rule, to allow FAA and industry users access to relevant rules and all active and superseded guidance material and related documents. This recommendation for creating the master source guidance system is the top priority of the Regulatory Consistency Committee. FAA officials indicated that establishing this system will require two main components: |

- As a first step, for linking (mapping) all relevant guidance materials to the regulations, FAA plans to determine which "guidance" documents exist across regional and field offices—including orders, notices, and advisory circulars—outside FAA's electronic guidance libraries, which are being used to answer questions, interpret or analyze regulations, and provide guidance on regulatory matters. In December 2013, Flight Standards sent out a memorandum requesting that staff discontinue using any guidance documents outside those found in the guidance libraries, to be effective January 15, 2014. The memorandum also asked for the staff to submit any unofficial guidance worth preserving to FAA for review. Flight Standards then conducted a review to determine which of the unofficial guidance documents submitted should be added to the guidance libraries. Several members of the Regulatory Consistency Committee responded in an e-mail to FAA to express serious concerns about this approach and stated that the committee did not envision the cancellation of any guidance before FAA developed a methodology to include or exclude such guidance. The committee members further noted that FAA's memorandum provided no method to allow existing certificate holders to retain certifications that were based on any applied guidance that had been cancelled. Further, these members requested that FAA either withdraw the memorandum or address the issues they raised and extend the date for FAA staff to comply with the memorandum. However, two other Regulatory Consistency Committee members we interviewed considered FAA's actions to get staff to discontinue the use of unofficial guidance in the field to be an appropriate first step.

- Second, FAA plans to develop a master source guidance system with the capability to consolidate information from Aircraft Certification's and Flight Standards' electronic guidance libraries as well as legal interpretations from the Office of Chief Counsel into a master guidance system to allow FAA and industry users access. Specifically, the Regulatory Consistency Committee recommended that this system be searchable so that FAA and industry users can easily access relevant rules and find the relevant guidance for the rule. FAA officials assessed the possibility of using the existing Aviation Safety Information Management System, but determined that it is not adequate because (1) users cannot search for guidance by word and (2) it is not compatible with other FAA data systems. According to FAA officials, with about $750,000 in approved funding for this project, FAA's information technology division is in the process of developing a dynamic regulatory system that should provide the needed capabilities. Officials indicated that when users conduct a search for a particular topic in this system, the search results should bring up multiple entries for specific guidance. Initially, Flight Standards plans to use an Excel spreadsheet for storing the guidance and then transition to the new system once it is deployed. Flight Standards hopes to test out a first version of this system within calendar year 2014. However, the officials were unsure of the total cost of developing and deploying the system.

Representatives from four of the committee stakeholders we interviewed for this testimony acknowledged that creating this system is a major effort for FAA because of the volume of FAA guidance that potentially exists across regional and field offices, some of which may not be in Aircraft Certification's and Flight Standards' electronic guidance libraries. Representatives of five industry stakeholders we interviewed provided insights on how FAA might devise a plan for creating and populating this system. Three of these noted that FAA will need to ensure that the various types of guidance—such as orders, notices, and advisory circulars—include links to the original federal aviation regulations. One of these stakeholders recommended that FAA develop the system to allow a user looking at FAA guidance to also see all relevant background information on related decisions, and the past actions related to the guidance in question and their relation to the original regulation. Because of the large volume of FAA guidance, some stakeholders also suggested that FAA begin by first choosing a starting date for which any new rules or other new guidance it issues would include links to the relevant original regulations. However, one stakeholder we interviewed noted that FAA should consider prioritizing its effort by first mapping the guidance materials for specific key regulations and then the guidance for less significant regulations.

Instructional Tools for FAA Personnel for Applying Policy and Guidance	The Regulatory Consistency Committee noted multiple instances where FAA guidance appeared to have created inconsistent interpretation and application, and confusion; the Consistency Committee recommended that FAA develop a standardized decision-making methodology for the development of all policy and guidance material to ensure such documents are consistent with adopted regulations. In interviews for this testimony, FAA officials also provided some updates on how the agency will respond to the recommendation to develop instructional tools for its policy staff. FAA officials told us they had not initiated any efforts yet to address this recommendation, but would begin by focusing on developing instructions for policy staff to use for populating the master source guidance system. In August 2014, FAA plans to form an internal work group to establish a document management framework and work processes that can be used by Aircraft Certification's and Flight Standards' policy division staffs as they map existing guidance documents to applicable source regulations in the master source guidance system. The officials expected the work group would issue an internal directive for FAA personnel on work processes to be used in populating the guidance system by June of 2015.
FAA and Industry Training Priorities and Curriculums	The Regulatory Consistency Committee recommended that FAA, in consultation with industry stakeholders, review and revise its regulatory training for applicable agency personnel and make the curriculum available to industry. FAA officials told us that FAA has begun to develop improved training for its field staff—the third recommendation of the Regulatory Consistency Committee—so that field inspector staffs are better equipped to answer routine compliance-related questions confidently and in a consistent manner. In addition, the officials told us starting in 2015, FAA plans to conduct a gap analysis of existing training for all FAA staff who are responsible for interpreting and applying certification and approval regulations. For this analysis, FAA plans to assess whether existing training can be modified to sufficiently address any gaps. FAA also plans to coordinate with industry to share the results of this review and analysis by the end of 2015.
Regulatory Consistency Communications Board	The Regulatory Consistency Committee made two similar recommendations for FAA to consider: (1) establish a Regulatory Consistency Communications Board comprising various FAA representatives that would provide clarification on questions from FAA and industry stakeholders related to the application of regulations and (2)

determine the feasibility of establishing a full-time Regulatory Operations Communication Center[27] as a centralized support center to provide real-time guidance to FAA personnel and industry certificate/approval holders and applicants. FAA officials also discussed the agency's conceptual approach and plans for establishing a board—likely by the end of calendar year 2014—to address these two recommendations. The purpose of the board would be to provide a neutral and centralized mechanism with a standardized process for addressing and resolving regulatory compliance issues between FAA and industry. According to the committee, this board would be comprised of representatives from the relevant headquarters policy divisions in FAA to help answer complex regulatory interpretation issues that arise between FAA inspectors and engineers, and industry during the certification and approval processes. FAA officials told us the board's process, once established, would use a modified version of the agency's current Consistency and Standardization Initiative (CSI), a process established as a means for industry to appeal FAA decisions and actions.

As we found in 2010, resolution through the CSI can be a lengthy process, with the total length of the process depending on how many levels of appeal the industry stakeholder chooses.[28] However, as we also found, industry stakeholders have generally been reluctant to use CSI for initiating appeals and raising concerns with the local field office for fear of retribution. FAA officials told us in interviews that the modified process would help address the retribution issue, because it would rely instead on multiple sources to raise issues—not just solely on industry—and would be the final arbiter for FAA and industry in disagreements on certification and approval decisions. According to FAA officials, the board could also serve the function of the proposed operations center recommended by the committee to be a resource for assisting FAA personnel and industry stakeholders with interpretation queries and establishing consistency in regulatory application. FAA officials indicated that the agency had decided not to establish the communications center because (1) the

[27]Under this operations center concept, FAA would establish a 24-hour/7-day operations center staffed (virtually) by policy and/or legal personnel trained and experienced in the regulations, policy and guidance associated with flight operations, aircraft maintenance, aircraft certification and aircraft production.

[28]GAO-11-14.

board could serve a similar function and (2) FAA has limited resources available to staff a communications center.

Several industry stakeholders we spoke with told us they support FAA's preliminary plans to establish the board and modify the CSI process as part of this effort. For example, several stakeholders told us that they support FAA's plans to modify the current CSI process. One of these stakeholders noted that a modified process would be more effective if it allowed for industry stakeholders to raise issues anonymously. Also, another stakeholder noted the board would not be beneficial until after FAA has established the master source guidance system because the board should be able to refer to that guidance in demonstrating how it makes decisions.

Clarity in Final Rules

The Regulatory Consistency Committee recommended that FAA improve the clarity of its final rules by ensuring that each final rule contains a comprehensive explanation of the rule's purpose and how it will increase safety. FAA officials told us that this recommendation has been addressed through the work of the Aviation Rulemaking Advisory Committee's Rulemaking Prioritization Working Group.[29] The officials told us that, as a result of this effort, all final rules, are now well-vetted across FAA. The industry representatives we interviewed had mixed opinions about whether FAA had addressed this recommendation as intended. For example, two stakeholders were in agreement with FAA that the agency had addressed it while two other stakeholders noted that FAA's new rules are still not as clear as they should be. Two stakeholders also said that it is often not the final rules but the guidance that accompanies or follows the final rules that is unclear and contributes to inconsistent interpretation and application among FAA staff.

---

[29]Specifically, in January 2013, FAA accepted the recommendation of the Rulemaking Prioritization Working Group that FAA should adopt a prioritization model across its lines of business for prioritizing rulemaking projects. In response, as we reported in prior work, FAA developed a tool that provides a standardized basis for evaluating and prioritizing potential rulemaking projects to be used by each line of business. See GAO-13-657.

Challenges that Could Affect Successful Implementation of the Committees' Recommendations

In our previous work on organizational transformations, we noted that implementing large-scale change management initiatives—like those the committees tasked FAA with—are not simple endeavors and require the concentrated efforts of both leadership and employees to realize intended synergies and accomplish new organizational goals.[30] People are at the center of any serious change management initiative because people define the organization's culture, drive its performance, and embody its knowledge base. The best approach for these types of initiatives depends upon a variety of factors specific to each context, but there has been some general agreement on a number of key practices that have consistently been found at the center of successful change management initiatives. These include, among other things, securing organizational support at all levels, developing clear principles and priorities to help change the culture, communicating frequently with partners, and setting performance measures to evaluate progress.[31] In this final section of this testimony, we discuss challenges for FAA in implementing the committees' certification and approval and regulatory consistency recommendations that relate to these key practices.

Organizational Support

FAA officials and industry representatives we spoke to noted that shifting priorities as well as declining resources may prohibit FAA from devoting the time and resources needed for completing the initiatives in the planned time frames. They agreed that a primary challenge for FAA will be having the dedicated resources that will be needed to successfully implement the committees' recommendations. We have previously found that successful organizational transformations and cultural changes require several years of focused attention from the agency's senior leadership.[32] This lesson is consistent with our previous work on organizational transformation, which indicates that support from top leadership is indispensable for fundamental change. Top leadership's clear and personal involvement in the transformation represents stability

---

[30]GAO, *Results-Oriented Cultures: Implementation Steps to Assist Mergers and Organizational Transformations*, GAO-03-669 (Washington, D.C: July 2, 2003).

[31]GAO-03-669, and GAO, *VA Health Care: Additional Efforts to Better Assess Joint Ventures Needed*, GAO-08-399 (Washington, D.C.: Mar. 28, 2008).

[32]GAO, *National Airspace System: Transformation Will Require Cultural Change, Balanced Funding Priorities, and Use of All Available Management Tools*, GAO-06-154 (Washington, D.C.: Oct. 14, 2005).

for both the organization's employees and its external partners. Top leadership must set the direction, pace, and tone for the transformation. Additionally, buy-in and acceptance among the workforce will be critical to successful implementation of the initiatives to address the two committees' recommendations.

Additionally, as we described in our 2010 report, FAA prioritizes ensuring the continued operational safety of the people and products already operating in the national airspace system over processing new certifications and approvals. We reported in the 2010 report that Flight Standards staff had little or no incentive to perform certification work under the system in which their pay grades are established and maintained.[33] Other than inspectors involved with overseeing air carriers, Flight Standards inspectors are typically responsible for a variety of types of certificate holders. Each certificate is allocated a point value based on the complexity of the certificate or operation, and the combined point value for each inspector's oversight responsibilities must meet or exceed the points allocated for the inspector's grade. However, not all of the inspectors' duties—including certification work—receive points in this system, and inspectors are subject to a downgrade if entities in their portfolio relocate or go out of business.

Commitment to Cultural Change

FAA and industry representatives also cited FAA's organizational culture as a primary challenge for FAA in successfully implementing these initiatives. They noted that many of the certification process and regulatory consistency initiatives FAA is attempting to implement represent cultural shifts for FAA staff in how regulations, policy, and guidance are applied, and ultimately how certification and approval decisions are made. As we have previously found, the implementation of recommendations that require a cultural shift for employees can be delayed if the workforce is reluctant in accepting such change.[34]

Communication with Stakeholders

Further, industry representatives have identified the lack of communication with and involvement of stakeholders as a primary challenge for FAA in implementing the committees' recommendations,

---

[33]GAO-11-14.

[34]GAO-14-142T.

particularly the regulatory consistency recommendations. Successful agencies we have studied based their strategic planning, to a large extent, on the interests and expectations of their stakeholders, and stakeholder involvement is important to ensure agencies' efforts and resources are targeted at the highest priorities.[35] However, representatives of two industry organizations we interviewed told us that FAA did not provide the opportunity for early input and that outreach is low regarding the certification process recommendations, and representatives of four industry organizations indicated that FAA has not sought their input in responding to the regulatory consistency recommendations. They reported that FAA had neither kept in contact with or advised them of its plans nor engaged the Regulatory Consistency Committee participants in the drafting of the detailed implementation plan that is expected to be published in August. As an example, as previously discussed, when Flight Standards published a memo in December 2013 calling for the cancellation of non-official guidance, several members of the Regulatory Consistency Committee were unaware of the change and expressed surprise and dissatisfaction with the action and offered their assistance. Representatives of one industry group noted that FAA sought their input on addressing the Certification Process Committee's recommendations for subsequent revisions of its implementation plan.

Setting Performance Measures

FAA has not fully developed performance metrics to ensure that any initiatives it implements are achieving their intended outcomes. We have previously found that agencies that have been successful in assessing performance use measures that demonstrate results and provide useful information for decision making.[36] Earlier in this testimony, we reported that FAA had not completed developing performance measures for either the certification improvement or the regulatory consistency initiatives:

- FAA had developed performance measures for 5 of the 14 certification process initiatives as of May 2014 and plans to further develop measures in three phases. In addition, most of the initiatives are scheduled to be implemented by 2017. Although we have

[35]GAO, *Executive Guide: Effectively Implementing the Government Performance and Results Act*, GAO/GGD-96-118 (Washington, D.C.: June 1, 1996).

[36]GAO, *NextGen Air Transportation System: FAA's Metrics Can be Used to Report on Status of Individual Programs, but Not of Overall NextGen Implementation or Outcomes*, GAO-10-629 (Washington, D.C.: July 27, 2010).

assessed FAA's plan for developing these metrics as reasonable, the agency may miss an opportunity to gather early data for evaluating the effectiveness of its actions and making any needed corrections.

- There is no detailed plan for implementing initiatives addressing the consistency of regulatory interpretation recommendations and measuring their outcomes. In recent meetings, FAA officials told us they have had difficulty in determining how to measure the outcomes of its regulatory consistency initiatives and have not been able to determine what specific performance metrics could be used.

Going forward, it is critically important that FAA develop outcome-based performance measures to determine what is actually being achieved through the current and future initiatives, thereby making it easier to determine the overall outcomes of each of the initiatives and to hold FAA's field and headquarters offices and employees accountable for the results. We are not making any new recommendations because the recommendation we made in 2010 for FAA to develop outcome-based performance measures and a continuous evaluative process continue to have merit related to this issue. To its credit, FAA has initiated some efforts and sound planning for addressing the committees' recommendations. However, it will be critical for FAA to follow through with its initiatives and plans for developing performance metrics to achieve the intended efficiencies and consistencies. As we noted in our October 2013 statement, however, some improvements to the certification and approval processes, will likely take years to implement and, therefore, will require a sustained commitment as well as congressional oversight.[37]

Chairman LoBiondo, Ranking Member Larsen, and Members of the Subcommittee, this completes my prepared statement. I would be pleased to respond to any questions at this time.

GAO Contact and Staff Acknowledgments

For further information on this testimony, please contact Gerald L. Dillingham, Ph.D., at (202) 512-2834 or dillinghamg@gao.gov. In addition, contact points for our Offices of Congressional Relations and Public Affairs may be found on the last page of this statement. Individuals

[37]GAO-14-142T.

making key contributions to this testimony statement include Vashun Cole, Assistant Director; Andrew Von Ah, Assistant Director; Jessica Bryant-Bertail; Jim Geibel; Josh Ormond; Amy Rosewarne; and Pamela Vines. The following individuals made key contributions to the prior GAO work: Teresa Spisak, Assistant Director; Melissa Bodeau, Sharon Dyer, Bess Eisenstadt, Amy Frazier, Brandon Haller, Dave Hooper, Sara Ann Moessbauer, and Michael Silver.